DISTINCT

LIVING ABOVE THE NORM

MICHAEL KELLEY

LifeWay Press® • Nashville, Tennessee

© 2015 LifeWay Press® • Reprinted 2016

ISBN 9781430034971 • Item 005680986

Dewey decimal classification: 248.84
Subject headings: CHRISTIAN LIFE \ CHARACTER \ DISCIPLESHIP

Eric Geiger
Vice President, LifeWay Resources

Ronnie Floyd
General Editor

Gena Rogers
Sam O'Neal
Content Editors

Michael Kelley
Director, Groups Ministry

Faith Whatley
Director, Adult Ministry

Printed in the United States of America

Send questions/comments to: Content Editor; *Bible Studies for Life: Adults*; One LifeWay Plaza; Nashville, TN 37234-0175; or make comments on the Web at *BibleStudiesforLife.com*.

For ordering or inquiries, visit *lifeway.com*; write to LifeWay Small Groups; One LifeWay Plaza; Nashville, TN 37234-0152; or call toll free 800.458.2772.

Bible Studies for Life: Adults often lists websites that may be helpful to our readers. Our staff verifies each site's usefulness and appropriateness prior to publication. However, website content changes quickly, so we encourage you to approach all websites with caution. Make sure sites are still appropriate before sharing them with students, friends, and family.

contents

7   Session 1   *Distinct in My Character*   *Matthew 5:1-12*

15   Session 2   *Distinct in My Influence*   *Matthew 5:13-20*

23   Session 3   *Distinct in My Approach to Conflict*   *Matthew 5:21-26*

31   Session 4   *Distinct in My Relationships*   *Matthew 5:27-32*

39   Session 5   *Distinct in My Reactions*   *Matthew 5:33-42*

47   Session 6   *Distinct in My Love*   *Matthew 5:43-48*

Leader Guide   *page 60*

Social Media

 Connect with a community of *Bible Studies for Life* users. Post responses to questions, share teaching ideas, and link to great blog content. ***Facebook.com/BibleStudiesForLife***

 Get instant updates about new articles, giveaways, and more. **@BibleMeetsLife**

The App

Simple and straightforward, this elegantly designed app gives you all the content of the Small Group Member Book—plus a whole lot more—right at your fingertips. Available in the iTunes App Store and for Android devices; search "**Bible Studies for Life**."

Blog

At ***BibleStudiesForLife.com/blog*** you will find magazine articles and music downloads from LifeWay Worship. Plus, leaders and group members alike will benefit from the blog posts written for people in every life stage—singles, parents, boomers, and senior adults—as well as media clips, connections between our study topics, current events, and much more.

Training

 For helps on how to use Bible Studies for Life, tips on how to better lead groups, or additional ideas for leading this session, visit: ***www.ministrygrid.com/web/biblestudiesforlife.***

ABOUT THIS STUDY

Don't blend. Don't compromise. *Be distinct.*

If everyone else jumped off a cliff, would you do it, too?

We all heard that one from our parents; some of us have even said it to our own kids. The point is simple: just because everyone else is doing something doesn't make it right. The problem, though, is that we like to fit in. Ever since we were kids, we wanted to like the right kind of music, wear the right clothes, and use the right technology.

In other words, we want to jump off the cliff *because* everyone else is doing it.

As disciples of Jesus, we were made to be different. To stand apart. To live in such a way that it's clear we aren't bandwagon crowd-followers; we're followers of Christ. That fact alone makes us stand apart— distinct from the crowd.

When we started following Jesus, everything about us changed, whether we recognized those changes or not. We have a new heart. We have new desires. We have new attitudes. And all of that newness stands in sharp contrast to the old.

In His most famous sermon, Jesus helped His followers—both then and now—see just how different God made us to be. In everything from our character to our relationships to the way we love other people, we were made to stand apart from the crowd. Just as it was for those who heard the Sermon on the Mount for the first time, every day of our lives is filled with opportunities for us to compromise and blend in with the norm.

Or to be distinct.

ABOUT THE AUTHOR

Michael Kelley

Michael Kelley is a husband, dad, author, and speaker. He serves as the Director of Groups at LifeWay Christian Resources and, in all those arenas, is trying to help people have a holistic view of what it means to be formed in Jesus. Michael is the author of *Boring: Finding an Extraordinary God in an Ordinary Life* and *Wednesdays Were Pretty Normal*, which tells the story of his 10-year-old son's battle with leukemia. Michael blogs at *michaelkelleyministries.com*.

DISTINCT IN MY CHARACTER

What was the happiest time in your life?

Choose actions and attitudes that are blessed by God.

THE BIBLE MEETS LIFE

You are being manipulated hundreds of times every day.

We typically don't use that label, but that's exactly what happens every time you watch a commercial, read a billboard, or get an Internet pop-up ad. Each and every one of those messages is trying to convince your subconscious mind of two things:

1. You are not as happy as you could be (or should be).

2. You will be happier if you drive this car, watch this show, buy this product, and so on.

It makes sense that marketers and advertisers go after our happiness. Who doesn't want to be happy? But what if being "happy" isn't the ultimate goal? What if there's something better?

As we'll see in today's Scripture focus, Jesus told His followers what life in His kingdom will be like. Will it be "happy"? Not exactly. It will be something far better. It will be "blessed."

WHAT DOES THE BIBLE SAY?

Matthew 5:1-12

1 When He saw the crowds, He went up on the mountain, and after He sat down, His disciples came to Him.

2 Then He began to teach them, saying:

3 "The poor in spirit are blessed, for the kingdom of heaven is theirs.

4 Those who mourn are blessed, for they will be comforted.

5 The gentle are blessed, for they will inherit the earth.

6 Those who hunger and thirst for righteousness are blessed, for they will be filled.

7 The merciful are blessed, for they will be shown mercy.

8 The pure in heart are blessed, for they will see God.

9 The peacemakers are blessed, for they will be called sons of God.

10 Those who are persecuted for righteousness are blessed, for the kingdom of heaven is theirs.

11 "You are blessed when they insult and persecute you and falsely say every kind of evil against you because of Me.

12 Be glad and rejoice, because your reward is great in heaven. For that is how they persecuted the prophets who were before you."

Blessed (v. 3)—The word "blessed" literally meant to be fortunate, happy, or joyful as a result of circumstances, or even more significantly here, as a result of and with emphasis on divine favor.

Poor in spirit (v. 3)—"Poor" primarily meant economically disadvantaged; symbolically, it meant lacking in spiritual significance or being inferior. Combined with "in spirit," the phrase is synonymous with being humble.

Matthew 5:1-6

This sermon is like a grenade tossed into the bunker of what we think it means to be happy in today's culture. The poor in spirit are blessed. Those who mourn are blessed. The gentle are blessed. Those who hunger and thirst for righteousness are blessed.

According to Jesus, being blessed is more than just happiness; it goes deeper than ordinary emotion and it's driven by more than mere circumstance. While the people in Jesus' day—like people in our own day—might have thought blessing came from being healthy, wealthy, and wise, understanding what true blessing means is one of the things that makes Christians distinct. Enduring happiness, or blessedness, comes with a life lived in a way that pleases God.

These first four qualities have to do more with a person's character than with his circumstances:

▶ **The poor in spirit.** These individuals know they are dependent on God for everything; they trust Him to provide what they need—even the grace they need to stand before Him.

▶ **Those who mourn.** Mourning can be done for all kinds of reasons. We might mourn over the state of the world or over the sin we see in our own lives. When we look around us—and within us—and mourn, we are blessed because we look to the comfort only God can bring.

▶ **The gentle.** In the kingdom of the world, the people who appear to inherit the earth are the go-getters and the ladder-climbers. But in God's kingdom, the gentle—those who submit themselves before God—inherit the whole earth.

▶ **Those who hunger and thirst.** These people are longing for righteousness. They look to God to satisfy their need, knowing true righteousness only comes from Him.

The blessed people Jesus described are those who know they need God and depend on Him; they are not satisfied with the temporary blessings of the world. The blessed Christian stands apart and distinct as he or she finds true satisfaction in what only God can provide.

Re Matt 5:
having been given
a precious gift by
God which should
bring joy

> **What is your understanding of what it means to be blessed?**

QUESTION #2

FEELING BLESSED

What are the major blessings in your life? Use the space below to record as many blessings as you can think of in a couple of minutes.

Christ / God / Salvation

Church / Fellowship

Myke

Nothan

Karen

Stephanie

Prayer

home & al

clothes

Nutrition

Slim figure

Monetary supply

cat? +/-

friends

work / truth

Natural & architectural beauty

What does your list of blessings communicate about your life?

God & people centred

beauty & comfort & security important to me.

Matthew 5:7-9

The cross on the right illustrates life in the kingdom of God. The vertical bar reflects our relationship with God. When we recognize our spiritual poverty, mourn over our sin, gently submit to Jesus as Savior and Lord, and hunger and thirst for His righteousness—our vertical relationship with God is realigned, and all is well between God and us. But it doesn't stop there.

Our vertical relationship with God impacts our horizontal relationships with others. If we truly experience the blessing of finding God's love and acceptance through Jesus, then that blessing is naturally reflected in our horizontal relationships.

In verses 3-6, Jesus described the kind of person who is blessed vertically—in his or her relationship with God. These next attributes show us what happens in horizontal relationships as a result:

▶ **The merciful.** The merciful don't seek revenge. Instead, they operate with a forgiving and gracious spirit. Human hurts pale in comparison to all that God has forgiven us.

▶ **The pure in heart.** The temptation is to act one way at home, a different way at work, and still another way at church. The blessed, however, are pure in heart. Every aspect of their lives displays steadfast purity and integrity.

▶ **The peacemakers.** Peacemaking takes a willingness to admit when you're wrong. It takes a humble spirit and the confidence to let things go—even when you might be right.

When we choose these attitudes toward other people, we stand in sharp distinction to the world. While so many are chasing their own happiness at the expense of others, true blessing is found in giving ourselves for the sake of others.

> *When have you felt the cost of choosing to show mercy, be pure, or make peace?*
>
> QUESTION #3

[handwritten note at top: Excluded from worldly parties... jobs, promotions, even whole careers, investments, martyrs, martyrs by family, rejected by family]

> **What are some ways Christians experience persecution in today's world?**

QUESTION #4

Matthew 5:10-12

This is the first time in these verses that Jesus gave a command. That's because all of these characteristics are representative of something that's happened inside us. When we come to Christ, we are fundamentally changed at the deepest level imaginable. We are citizens in a new kingdom, and in that kingdom we have new values and new definitions.

In other words, we are citizens in God's kingdom, but we still live in this world. So Jesus commanded us in verse 12: "Be glad and rejoice."

We can't always control how we feel. We become angry, sad, or nervous, but we don't have to stay mired in those emotions. We can make the choice—no matter what the circumstances are—to rejoice and be glad. We must remind ourselves of the truth despite what we might feel. That's why "rejoice" is a command instead of a feeling.

Tell yourself who's Boss. *Jesus is Lord of my life, and He is Lord over all.* Because of that truth, we can choose to rejoice and be glad despite the tough stuff of life. We make an active choice to stand against the current of our circumstances and choose joy.

Jesus also gave us a check to make sure we're rejoicing in the right thing. He reminded us that we can choose to rejoice about what really matters. Those who go against the world's current stand out clearly. They are distinct from the world. They are more than happy—they are blessed.

[handwritten note: Quote Matt 5:10-12? pray give $$]

> **How do we help one another choose joy when others mistreat us because of our faith?**

QUESTION #5

LIVE IT OUT

What steps will you take this week to seek our blessing rather than mere happiness? Consider the following suggestions:

▶ **Allow God's Word to bless you.** Memorize Matthew 5:3-6 and pray through Jesus' words every day.

▶ **Bless someone else by serving them.** Choose one relationship this week in which you want to model what it means to be blessed. Serve that person in a tangible way.

▶ **Allow someone else to bless you.** Share with someone you trust about a tough situation you are walking through. Ask him or her to help you choose to be glad and rejoice in the middle of that situation.

Christians are different; they are distinct. They display that distinction in their dependence on God, their actions toward others, and the way they respond to difficulties.

So, are you ready to find something bigger than happiness?

My thoughts

DISTINCT IN MY INFLUENCE

What flavoring or spice could you not live without?

QUESTION #1

Make your influence count for what matters.

THE BIBLE MEETS LIFE

I'm convinced very few people in the world really like trail mix. We say we do, but most of us really only eat trail mix for one reason: the M&M's®. Trail mix offers a way to eat candy and feel healthy at the same time, since the ingredients are all mixed together.

Like a bag of trail mix, believers in Christ are mixed into the world. And like the candy in the trail mix, Christians must retain their distinctiveness even while mixed into all other kinds of life situations.

I've noticed a funny thing about trail mix. Even though all different kinds of things are in the bag, they all end up tasting just a little bit like chocolate. The sweetness has flavored everything else. Like that sweet chocolate, Christians aren't meant to simply be in the mix of the culture, or even to stand out in the mix; they're meant to influence the world around them.

As Jesus continued the Sermon on the Mount, He gave us some illustrations of how this influence happens.

WHAT DOES THE BIBLE SAY?

Matthew 5:13-20

13 "You are the salt of the earth. But if the salt should lose its taste, how can it be made salty? It's no longer good for anything but to be thrown out and trampled on by men.

14 "You are the light of the world. A city situated on a hill cannot be hidden.

15 No one lights a lamp and puts it under a basket, but rather on a lampstand, and it gives light for all who are in the house.

16 In the same way, let your light shine before men, so that they may see your good works and give glory to your Father in heaven.

17 "Don't assume that I came to destroy the Law or the Prophets. I did not come to destroy but to fulfill.

18 For I assure you: Until heaven and earth pass away, not the smallest letter or one stroke of a letter will pass from the law until all things are accomplished.

19 Therefore, whoever breaks one of the least of these commands and teaches people to do so will be called least in the kingdom of heaven. But whoever practices and teaches these commands will be called great in the kingdom of heaven.

20 For I tell you, unless your righteousness surpasses that of the scribes and Pharisees, you will never enter the kingdom of heaven."

The Law or the Prophets (v. 17)—Shorthand for the Old Testament. The prominence of the books of the Law (Genesis–Deuteronomy) and Prophets (Isaiah, Jeremiah, Ezekiel, etc.) made it a suitable abbreviation.

Not the smallest letter or one stroke of a letter (v. 18)—The Greek letter *iota* translates the Hebrew letter *yod,* the smallest letter in the Hebrew alphabet. The Greek term *keraia* (stroke) means "horn" or "hook" and refers to small, decorative marks added to Hebrew letters.

Matthew 5:13

God intends for us to stride through life with confidence, retaining our uniqueness as His people while influencing those around us. To illustrate this, Jesus likened His followers to salt.

▶ **Salt seasons.** It's amazing what a pinch of salt can do to bring out the flavor inside food. Similarly, when Christians exert their influence in the world, we season the world with the gospel of Christ. Throughout history, we see how this has happened as followers of Jesus have contributed to the overall good of cultures and societies. God has used His people to extend His love to the world in amazing ways. In fact, most major social innovations—health care, education, and programs to assist the poor and hungry—have been the result of Christians "seasoning" the environment in which they live.

▶ **Salt preserves.** People in Jesus' day used salt to help preserve their food. Salt kept the food from going bad and enabled it to last longer. When Christians exert their influence in everyday situations, they keep the world from getting worse than it already is. Christians display integrity, goodness, honesty, and joy; in doing so, they hold up a society whose trajectory is headed lower and lower.

▶ **Salt makes you thirsty.** Salty food makes you crave water to quench your thirst. Whether people sense it or not, they are thirsty for something more. When Christians exert their influence and display the goodness and joy they have found to be uniquely satisfying, it salts the palate of everyone else. Suddenly, they become more aware that something is missing in their lives. When people in the world see how followers of Christ respond to life, what the believers have in Christ—and the difference it makes in their lives—rises to the surface. And it makes people thirsty. Christians in turn are ready to show them the way to Jesus, the fountain of life that never runs out (see John 4:14; 7:37-38).

> *Salt flavors and preserves. How do Christians both preserve and improve culture?*

QUESTION #2

By living godly lives of purity & love.
Loving with action & truth.
Being different but also present.

LIGHT OF THE WORLD

How do you picture serving as the light of the world? Select one of the following images that best represents what it means for you to shine the light of Christ. Or, use the blank box to draw your own.

culture blurs my light w. family & non-christian world.

What obstacles prevent you from shining the light of Christ more brightly?

Fatigue. Lack of emotional tensile strength. Family responsibilities keep me from public ministries. I can shine, but not prominently.

So I am not in a peck-measure, but I am on a table in a small room.

Matthew 5:14-16

Jesus told His followers, "I am the light of the world" (John 8:12). But why did He choose to compare Himself to light? Consider the purpose of light. In that day and time, light wasn't meant to decorate a house; no one had a lamp sitting around because it looked pretty. Light was about utility and work; it existed in a limited supply, and it was important that people make the most of the time while the light was still shining. That's because only in the light can we really see and know the true nature of what's before us.

When you light a lamp in a darkened room, you get immediate clarity. Without the light, mystery, apprehension, and even fear controls the scene; you can't truly identify where or what anything is. But light reveals. It shows us the truth about what otherwise is hidden in darkness. That's exactly what Jesus does.

Jesus exposed a lot of things that had been in the dark for a long time. He shined the light on the hypocrisy of the religious leaders of the day. He refused to accept half-hearted devotion to God. He called sin "sin," and He extended love and truth with His whole self.

In these verses, Jesus extended the idea of lighting the world to His followers. Like Him, His followers are meant to light the world—and to light it brightly. As weary travelers look with hope to the bright and warm city on the hill, so the world should look to Christians to tell the truth and welcome them warmly into God's kingdom.

But God's light and truth are not always easy. With light comes truth, but the truth is not always comfortable. Being the light of the world means we must stand for truth even when others pressure us not to. Jesus was the light, and it cost His life. We shouldn't be surprised when being the light costs us, as well. Jesus warned against the temptation to dampen the bright light within us.

> *Give to organizations that minister in the name of the Lord.*
>
> *Find ways to offer appreciation to God.*

> **How do we shine our light in a way that brings glory to God and not ourselves?**
>
> QUESTION #3

Matthew 5:17-20

When Jesus burst onto the scene, people had a lot of questions about who He was and what He came to do. He wasn't like any teacher they'd heard before. He performed miracles. He associated with the kinds of people that were generally considered off limits. And He taught with authority.

In that day and time, a teacher would establish his authority by boasting about his résumé. He would announce who his teacher was and what that rabbi said about an issue. In contrast, Jesus said, "You have heard that it was said … but I tell you …." (See vv. 21-22, for example.) Jesus is authoritative in and of Himself; He doesn't need anyone else to establish His credibility. Jesus is His own résumé.

At the same time, Jesus said, "not the smallest letter or one stroke of a letter will pass from the law until all things are accomplished" (v. 18). Jesus didn't replace the written Word of God; He fulfilled it. That's because the law was never intended to be the means to make people right with God. Instead, it was always meant to point people to Jesus.

Verse 20 can seem confusing. How can we have righteousness that "surpasses that of the scribes and Pharisees"? We can't. But Jesus did, and He gives it to us. When we receive Jesus' righteousness, we are changed on the inside. What's left for us, then, is to live out the change Jesus has brought to our hearts. We do this through our loving obedience. Those who live out this grace-filled change are like salt. And light. They influence others by visibly demonstrating what Jesus has done in their hearts.

> **When has the Bible sparked your ability to live as salt and light?**

QUESTION **#4**

> **What's one step you can take this week to live as salt and light in your community?**

QUESTION **#5**

[handwritten note] Ro 6
2 b: How can we who died to sin still live in it? ... 14 for sin will have no dominion over you since you are not under law but under grace.

[handwritten note] ← ? See next page.

[handwritten note] 15. What then, are we to sin because we are not under law but under grace? By no means!

LIVE IT OUT

How will you serve as salt and light in your world this week? Consider the following suggestions:

▶ **Pray for the darkness.** Christians often complain about the darkness in our world—but that accomplishes nothing. Instead, commit to praying each day when you encounter elements of society that need to experience the salt and light of Christ.

▶ **Don't go it alone.** Identify a believer in Christ whom you respect—someone who uses his or her influence in a positive way. Ask to meet with that person to help you follow Jesus more closely.

▶ **Speak up.** Look for a chance this week to speak directly about the gospel at a place outside your church or Bible study group.

We're all mixed together in this world, which means everyone has the chance to influence everyone else. The question is how we'll use the opportunities we've been given. Choose to be salt and light.

My thoughts

DISTINCT IN MY APPROACH TO CONFLICT

When have you regretted settling for a quick fix?

QUESTION #1

#BSFLdistinct

Take the lead in resolving conflict.

THE BIBLE MEETS LIFE

Imagine coming onto the scene of an auto accident. Two cars so twisted around each other, you think to yourself, *There's no way anyone survived this.*

But then you see someone sitting in the back of the ambulance. He's alive, but you can tell something is terribly wrong. He winces in pain every time he moves. The last thing you'd expect the paramedic to do is place a Band-Aid on the man's elbow, slap him on the back, and say, "You're good to go, buddy."

What?!

Just because you don't see an injury on the surface doesn't mean something critical isn't going on deep inside. In other words, you don't put a Band-Aid on internal hemorrhaging.

As Jesus continued to teach through His Sermon on the Mount, He came to the subject of anger. But anger isn't just a surface issue. Like everything else in Jesus' sermon, anger is a matter of the heart.

WHAT DOES THE BIBLE SAY?

Matthew 5:21-26

21 "You have heard that it was said to our ancestors, Do not murder, and whoever murders will be subject to judgment.

22 But I tell you, everyone who is angry with his brother will be subject to judgment. And whoever says to his brother, 'Fool!' will be subject to the Sanhedrin. But whoever says, 'You moron!' will be subject to hellfire.

23 So if you are offering your gift on the altar, and there you remember that your brother has something against you,

24 leave your gift there in front of the altar. First go and be reconciled with your brother, and then come and offer your gift.

25 Reach a settlement quickly with your adversary while you're on the way with him, or your adversary will hand you over to the judge, the judge to the officer, and you will be thrown into prison.

26 I assure you: You will never get out of there until you have paid the last penny!"

Fool (v. 22)—This word comes from the Aramaic term *rhaka* [RAH kuh]. This insult refers to an idiot or empty-headed person, meaning someone mentally inept.

Moron (v. 22)—This word derives from the Greek term *moros,* and is primarily translated as "fool" or some variation or related form of that word.

Be careful to keep peace!

> **What's your initial reaction to these verses?**
>
> QUESTION **#2**

Matthew 5:21-22

Does verse 22 make you uncomfortable? Me too.

Jesus took a law the people knew well and expanded it to a different level. The original commandment was a prohibition against taking someone's life (see Ex. 20:13). That's easy enough to grasp. But Jesus wasn't content to settle for the physical act of murder; the deeper issue is the anger we feel in our hearts. Furthermore, Jesus helps us see that anger isn't something that happens to us; it's a choice we make. We might not be able to control the circumstances around us, but it's ultimately our choice whether or not we respond to those circumstances with anger.

It's not always wrong to be angry. At times Jesus Himself became righteously angry. For example, He became angry when the religious leaders failed to show compassion for a man with a withered hand (see Mark 3:1-5). Later, Jesus became so enraged at the mistreatment of people seeking to worship that He turned over the money changers' tables and ran them out of His Father's house (see John 2:13-16).

A certain kind of anger is good, right, and justified. We feel that righteous anger when we see injustice in the world. Whenever we feel righteous indignation because others are mistreated, we aren't only justified in our anger; we are good and right in doing something constructive with that anger.

But that assumes that our hearts are aligned with God's heart. Most of the time, though, that's not the case. We get angry at the slow-moving traffic or the child who has to be told to clean up his toys for the thousandth time. This isn't righteous anger.

Let me ask the really hard question: *Why do we get angry?*

If we push past the circumstances, we'll discover the true reason we get angry is because we feel our rights have been violated. *I should be treated better. I deserve more.* The truth is, our anger stems from a deeply held sense of entitlement that, when crossed, makes us really, really mad.

In other words, our anger is a reflection of our commitment to ourselves.

PERSONAL ASSESSMENT: ANGER

Do you have an anger problem? Use the following assessments to evaluate how quickly, and how completely, you give in to anger.

How long does it take you to feel angry during a difficult or offensive situation?

Reverse racism ↓

O————————O————————O————————O————————●

(hours)   (seconds)

How often in a typical month do you feel something close to rage?

◉————————O————————O————————O————————●

(zero times)   (more than five times)

When was the last time you deeply regretted actions taken or words spoken in anger?

O————————O————————O————————O————————●

(years ago)   *impatience,* (days ago)
                                          not anger.

last summer I showed
how offended I was re reverse racism.
In that case I should have let it go?

When was the last time a close friend or family member confessed to feeling afraid of you?

O————————O————————O————————O————————●

(years ago)   (days ago)

never.

"There is nothing that can be done with anger that cannot be done better without it!"

—DALLAS WILLARD

Matthew 5:23-24

"I'm sorry." Those are painful words. They're so painful, in fact, we often qualify them by adding one more little word that changes everything: "I'm sorry, but … ."

That's not being sorry. That's choosing the road of self-justification. We say this when we want the other person to know that, even though we lashed out in anger or did something wrong, we had a justified reason for our behavior.

Anger often leads to conflict. Conflict often leads to relationships being strained to the breaking point—and beyond. It's in those moments that we need to remember Jesus' amazing statement from verse 24: reconciliation takes priority over worship. That's serious.

Even more, we are to be proactive in resolving conflict. We should take the first step, even when we aren't to blame for the conflict in the first place. How can we do that?

1. **Honesty.** Be willing to hear—and tell—the truth. Don't be tempted to treat this like an airing of dirty laundry. The truth is useful for healing, but it's not intended to be used as a hammer to beat the other person over the head.

2. **Humility.** In most conflicts, both sides have things they need to acknowledge and apologize for. In order to do so, you must have a humble heart. Humility will help you forgive with the same grace and mercy God forgave you.

3. **Security.** Security doesn't mean arrogance. It means knowing you are a child of God. When you are secure and confident in your relationship with Jesus, you can apologize. How the person responds to your apology or attempt to reconcile cannot change your secure relationship in Christ.

> *Reconciliation requires honesty, humility, and security. Which of these do you find challenging?*

QUESTION #3

if the other one is not ready to talk, you have to figure w/o talking.

> **What are some concrete principles Jesus established in this passage?**

QUESTION **#4**

Matthew 5:25-26

Jesus commanded us not to put off reconciliation; instead, we are to settle and resolve differences quickly. We see at least two reasons why resolution demands this degree of urgency:

▶ **Earlier is easier.** The earlier individuals can face and discuss their differences, the easier it will be to reach a resolution. Problems between people don't get better with time; they get worse.

▶ **Unity is important.** Resolution demands urgency because unity is vitally important among God's people. Just before He was arrested, Jesus prayed for all His followers, past and present. One of the resounding themes in this high priestly prayer was unity (see John 17).

Think about that for a minute. Jesus was only hours away from His death, praying to His Father, and unity in the church was on His mind. Why might that be?

The unity of God's people provides proof of the gospel. In the church, you find people of all different nationalities, races, backgrounds, and socioeconomic levels. All these people come together under the banner of Jesus Christ. No other organization can unite people who are so completely different.

When we let our differences fester and divide us, the rest of the world questions the effectiveness of the gospel. But the unity of the church points to the power of the gospel.

> **What are the consequences of allowing a conflict to fester?**

QUESTION **#5**

LIVE IT OUT

Anger is an issue of the heart. Consider the following suggestions as you work to bring your anger under the rule of Jesus in the days to come:

▶ **Take control of your anger.** You know what situations are likely to make you angry this week. Prepare your heart and mind to respond appropriately before you ever step into that situation.

▶ **Say you're sorry.** Look for a chance to say "I'm sorry" this week without qualification. Humble yourself before Christ and the other person, and say those two words that can bring healing.

▶ **Seek reconciliation.** Examine your relationships, past and present. Is there someone you still need to reconcile with? If so, don't wait any longer. Seek to honor Christ through the process of reconciliation.

Anger is a big deal in today's world, which is why I pray you'll let the words of Jesus sink into your heart. Don't put a Band-Aid on internal hemorrhaging. Look deeper to find the real source of your anger, and then reset the fracture so that you can heal.

My thoughts

DISTINCT IN MY RELATIONSHIPS

When was the last time you couldn't hear yourself think?

#BSFLdistinct

QUESTION #1

Hold on to purity at all costs.

THE BIBLE MEETS LIFE

The world's quietest room is at Orfield Laboratories in Minneapolis, MN. It's a chamber built with double walls of concrete and insulated steel covered by 3.3-foot thick acoustic fiberglass wedges. It's said that a person can hear his or her own beating heart, gurgling stomach, and even pulsing inner ear.

Most people can't take the silence for more than 30 minutes.

Our lives are filled with "noise," and we're often comfortable with that. But busy, noisy lives can keep us from hearing the truth of what's inside us. Greed, selfishness, lust, and a host of other things are hiding in our hearts.

When we recognize the dual threat of both the internal and the external, we see the gravity of God's call to live pure lives. It's not just a call to purity in terms of our actions, but in our very being. It's a call for absolute agreement in our thoughts, feelings, and actions.

WHAT DOES THE BIBLE SAY?

Matthew 5:27-32

27 "You have heard that it was said, Do not commit adultery.

28 But I tell you, everyone who looks at a woman to lust for her has already committed adultery with her in his heart.

29 If your right eye causes you to sin, gouge it out and throw it away. For it is better that you lose one of the parts of your body than for your whole body to be thrown into hell.

30 And if your right hand causes you to sin, cut it off and throw it away. For it is better that you lose one of the parts of your body than for your whole body to go into hell!

31 "It was also said, Whoever divorces his wife must give her a written notice of divorce.

32 But I tell you, everyone who divorces his wife, except in a case of sexual immorality, causes her to commit adultery. And whoever marries a divorced woman commits adultery."

A written notice of divorce (v. 31)—The Greek word translated here originally carried the sense of abandonment of property; then, in Jewish circles, the term acquired the meaning of a certificate of divorce given to a woman so she could remarry without charge of adultery.

Matthew 5:27-30

There's no doubt about it: sex is a powerful force in today's world. "Sex sells." But why?

The answer is that sex was designed to be the most pure, the most uninhibited, and the most unashamed kind of intimacy imaginable. God intended it to be an act in which a person is both known and fully knows another person without shame, holding nothing back. But, like everything else in the world, sex has been corrupted. Instead of serving as an expression of love and intimacy, sex has become a tool for personal gratification at the expense of another human being.

That brings us to the topic of purity. In Matthew 5, Jesus taught that true purity isn't just a matter of abstaining from sinful sex; it's a condition of the heart that must be corrected. He called us to engage in the fight for purity at any cost. In verses 29-30, He gave us a battle plan for pursuing that kind of purity:

▶ **Identify the source.** Jesus told us to root out the source of impurity. His vivid illustrations involved the eyes and the hand, but we might think about temptation in terms of other sources. Are you tempted by images you see on your computer or television? Does a certain relationship or habit trouble you? Do you struggle during a period of time you have to spend alone?

▶ **Deal ruthlessly with the temptation.** According to Jesus, if our eye causes us to sin, we should gouge it out. If it's our hand, we should cut it off. Though that might sound extreme, the reason is simple: When you consider what's at stake, you'll do whatever it takes to protect your purity. When you consider that these patterns of behavior, if left unchecked, cause you to fall under God's judgment, then you'll start taking them a little more seriously.

> *What are the dividing lines between "pure" and "impure" in today's world?*
>
> QUESTION #2

> *How can we be ruthless in resisting impurity without being judgmental and condemning?*
>
> QUESTION #3

What does the Holy Spirit be subjected to?

▶ **Replace the temptation with something better.** Don't focus on not thinking impure thoughts; focus instead on something better. Find something constructive to do for the kingdom with your time. Fill the void left by temptation with something more—something better—and soon you won't have to invest the mental energy to not think about whatever it was that caused you to struggle. It's been replaced.

SEEKING SOURCES

As sojourners in the modern world, we all face temptation from time to time.
Circle the words below that represent major sources of temptation in your life.

Entertainment

Television   Relationships   Isolation   (Possessions)   Popularity   (Internet)

politics

Control   Loneliness   Peer Pressure   Credit   Power   Pride   Food

Love/stress

What's one step you can take this week to distance yourself from
one of the temptation sources you circled above?

Pray like crazy?
• make a budget that controls purchases & adds giving.
• find a way to reduce time on politics & movies.

Matthew 5:31-32

God created our bodies, and He gave us our human needs and desires as integral parts of those bodies. God also gave us good and right avenues to fulfill those desires.

Sin happens when we seek to satisfy a God-given desire through an unholy avenue. Instead of turning to the God-given avenues of fulfilling those desires, we turn to whatever is easiest. Or most convenient. Or the least costly.

In verse 31, Jesus brought marriage into His discussion of purity. Marriage is the physical and spiritual union between a man and a woman for a lifetime; it is the one and only way God has given us to express and fulfill sexual desire.

Unfortunately, marriage—like sex—has fallen under the shadow of sin. God intended the marriage covenant to be a reflection of the covenant He makes with His own people and, therefore, to be unbroken. Because of sin, however, marriages have failed to live up to God's standard.

In verse 31, Jesus quoted from the Old Testament law (see Deut. 24:1). In this particular law, a man was required to produce a divorce certificate instead of just arbitrarily deciding he didn't want to be married anymore. This provision was instituted to provide legal protection for the divorced woman, since women had few rights in that culture and little ability to provide for themselves. Without this stipulation, a man could threaten to divorce his wife and leave her destitute.

Jesus

Whom do you look to as a model of faithfulness?

QUESTION #4

Even though the law was designed to protect women, the rabbis and religious leaders of Jesus' day had distorted this law to allow divorce for even minor complaints. What was designed to be good was being used to abuse.

model faithfulness & chastity

Jesus called us back to the sacred nature of marriage. He did give one exception, however. Divorce may be permitted if a spouse is unfaithful to the marriage. That doesn't mean Jesus condones divorce; in fact, it means the opposite. God loves and values marriage highly as a covenant relationship. A marriage can be ended only if someone is unfaithful. Faithfulness is so important that, if violated, God will allow a covenant that was established before Him to be ended.

What can we learn from these verses? Jesus is telling us to hold onto marriage. Commit to it. Don't run, but stay faithful. Keep the following in mind:

▶ **Marriage is difficult.** Marriage is difficult because we confront the depth of our selfishness. When we truly have to put someone else's needs ahead of our own, we discover where our commitments lie.

▶ **Marriage is supported.** No couple faces the challenges of marriage alone. God is with us, and God is for us. He is pro-marriage. In fact, He's so much in favor of marriage that He chose the relationship between a husband and a wife to represent His own relationship with His people (see Rev. 19:7-8; 21:2; 22:17).

▶ **Marriage is an opportunity for growth.** God uses difficulties within marriage to make us more like Jesus. Marriage, the most intimate relationship, is the ideal place to display and practice the fruit of the Spirit: love, joy, peace, patience, kindness, goodness, faith, gentleness, and self-control (see Gal. 5:22-23).

"It is human to err. It is devilish to remain willfully in error."

—ST. AUGUSTINE

LIVE IT OUT

Holding on to purity isn't always easy, but it's always valuable. Consider the following suggestions for seeking purity this week:

▶ **Replace.** What is one way you are spending your time that is not contributing to your personal purity? Look for something to replace it this week.

▶ **Serve.** Consider a practical way you can serve your spouse this week. For example, intentionally do the one thing around the house your spouse doesn't enjoy doing.

▶ **Talk.** Begin the process of accountability by letting your guard down with someone you trust. Initiate a conversation with that person and share one way in which you are struggling to hold on to purity at all costs.

You don't have to settle for the world's standard of purity and faithfulness. God has something more. Go after it.

My thoughts

DISTINCT IN MY REACTIONS

Nevec!

When have you felt like you were organized and on top of things?

QUESTION #1

#BSFLdistinct

Practice grace and integrity when others make demands of you.

THE BIBLE MEETS LIFE

Some of us live according to "to-do" lists. Time management folks tell us these are a great way to keep track of and prioritize the things we need to accomplish. The blessing of such a "to-do" list is that you have a target to shoot for. The curse of a "to-do" list is that it can remind you of what you didn't get accomplished—or what remains to be finished.

Unfinished "to-do" lists happen a lot. That's not because the tasks weren't important. It's because things pop up every day you simply didn't anticipate.

Interruptions.

We can't stop the interruptions or demands other people make in our lives. But how we react to those interruptions is completely in our hands. <u>Jesus is concerned about our reactions</u>. Why? Because the ways we react in irritating situations will—or won't—show us to be distinctly Christian. <u>Jesus calls us to a standard that is consistent, honest, and filled with grace.</u>

WHAT DOES THE BIBLE SAY?

Matthew 5:33-42

33 "Again, you have heard that it was said to our ancestors, You must not break your oath, but you must keep your oaths to the Lord.

34 But I tell you, don't take an oath at all: either by heaven, because it is God's throne;

35 or by the earth, because it is His footstool; or by Jerusalem, because it is the city of the great King.

36 Neither should you swear by your head, because you cannot make a single hair white or black.

37 But let your word 'yes' be 'yes,' and your 'no' be 'no.' Anything more than this is from the evil one.

38 "You have heard that it was said, An eye for an eye and a tooth for a tooth.

39 But I tell you, don't resist an evildoer. On the contrary, if anyone slaps you on your right cheek, turn the other to him also.

40 As for the one who wants to sue you and take away your shirt, let him have your coat as well.

41 And if anyone forces you to go one mile, go with him two.

42 Give to the one who asks you, and don't turn away from the one who wants to borrow from you."

His footstool (v. 35)—When used literally, this term refers to an actual footstool (see Jas. 2:3). Here, the term is used figuratively—God has no need of a place to rest His feet. Thus, it represents the earth's complete submission to God.

Swear by your head (v. 36)—It was a custom to guarantee the truthfulness of a statement by swearing or taking an oath by invoking God or some substitute for God; here, "your head" is that substitute.

Matthew 5:33-37

We've all felt the pain of a broken commitment or word. And we've all had our own share of failed commitments to others. It hurts in both directions.

As we continue with the Sermon on the Mount, we see Jesus pushing us to examine our integrity through the lens of our words and the promises we make. The Old Testament law repeatedly commanded people to keep their word and be absolutely truthful (see Lev. 19:12; Num. 30:2; Deut. 23:21-23). But by the time of Jesus, people were making distinctions in their promises and oaths: some were super serious, others were not so serious.

If someone made a promise using God's name, he was bringing God into the promise; thus, it became a serious promise he must keep. But if someone simply gave her own word on a matter, it was considered much less serious. Jesus made the point that God is always involved when a person gives his or her word. Whenever we make a promise, we are doing so in the presence of God.

Here are two things worth remembering:

▶ **Be careful what you commit to.** Many of us have a tendency to overcommit ourselves. We may have the best of intentions, but at some point we have to develop the discipline of saying no.

▶ **Keep your word when you give it.** God honors the person "who keeps his word whatever the cost" (Ps. 15:4). Unforeseen circumstances can pop up that make it difficult to keep some promises. Even when it hurts to do so, however, the one who keeps his promises pleases God.

What motivates us to say, "I promise?"

QUESTION **#2**

When someone doesn't trust us?

Signature

Matthew 5:38-39

The Old Testament records this "eye for an eye" law three times (see Ex. 21:23-24; Lev. 24:19-20; Deut. 19:21). But God's intention was to limit vengeance, not give license to it. The law was meant to make sure that conflict didn't escalate, but was kept within specific boundaries. Furthermore, the wronged individual was never to seek justice or vengeance on his own. Instead, the law served as a guide for judges as they decided appropriate punishments through court proceedings.

Jesus, however, reordered our thinking. He told us we are not to retaliate when we are humiliated or insulted.

Because we're born with the inclination of self-defense and retaliation, we are fighting against our sinful human nature when we follow Jesus in this distinct way. In other words, we must choose to deny ourselves in order to obey Jesus' commands.

▶ **We deny our rights.** People usually believe they have something coming to them when they're wronged. Yet Jesus called us to deny our "rights." We are to follow Him on the road of forgiveness and self-denial.

▶ **We deny our entitlement.** Closely akin to our rights is a sense of entitlement. Something rises up inside us that says, "I deserve better." But any feeling of entitlement fails to recognize that all we are truly entitled to is death and hell. We experience God's mercy and forgiveness because of His grace, not because we are entitled to them.

▶ **We deny our pride.** Often the worst part of what we experience at the hand of someone else is the blow to our ego. We feel humiliated and our pride is offended. We must let go of our inflated ego and release our pride in favor of following Jesus on the path of humility (see Phil. 2:5-8).

> *What are some practical ways to turn the other cheek in today's culture?*

QUESTION **#3**

Hints from other class members: talk gently. Use grace.

> *When do we cross the line between turning the other cheek and living as a victim?*

QUESTION **#4**

There are times to gracefully confront. There are times to stand up & not cower - but w. grace & love.

Matthew 5:40-42

As if it weren't enough to say we should not seek revenge when someone does us wrong, Jesus went the extra mile in His teaching. He said we should do the same thing—go the extra mile—even for those who want to take advantage of us. According to Jesus, we should overwhelm such people with kindness.

We tend to think about obedience in terms of minimums. What's the minimum amount of stuff I have to do to get by? That kind of attitude shows a heart out of touch with the grace God has lavished on us. Jesus' point is that we shouldn't focus on the minimum; instead, we should focus on how we can be a blessing to others.

To go the extra mile—above and beyond—takes more than willpower. It takes faith. We need to believe three things to go the extra mile:

▷ **Believe God will provide.** Going the extra mile is costly. It could be a coat; it could be some money; it could be our time. It will cost us something. We must believe in a God who will provide the coat, the money, or the time that we've given up for the sake of someone else.

▷ **Believe God will rectify.** When we give sacrificially for the sake of someone else, we might be tempted to treat it like a loan. We shouldn't. Much in the same way that we don't seek revenge because we believe God will set everything right in the end, we can freely go the extra mile without the expectation of payback. Trust in God, who knows what we've done.

▷ **Believe God will redeem.** What if we go the extra mile and nothing happens? What if the person doesn't recognize our gift or what it cost us? We might be tempted to become bitter and resentful, or to wish we never made the effort in the first place. But God redeems. Though it might seem like a waste at first, we trust God in His wisdom and power to redeem what we've done for His good purposes.

> *How do we prepare ourselves now to respond well when others make demands of us?*

QUESTION **#5**

[handwritten notes: Deny all money & resources to God - make Him owner. Love others lavishly. Remind self of God's goodness often]

Jesus' command to go the extra mile is countercultural in today's society. How would you respond to a friend or family member who made the following claims? Choose one.

"I have to look out for myself first and foremost, because no one else will."

> God will look after me. I will live & walk in love for my neighbor, with God's help.

"You can't let people take advantage of you in life. Whenever you give an inch, there are people ready to take a mile."

> Sew an action, reap a character.
> Sometimes it is better to be swindled than to become selfish. Sometimes it is better for the other person not to give — but love must guide.

"I have every right to be happy. I deserve it."

> why do you deserve it? What do you have that has not been given to you? What do you owe God compared to what you feel entitled to?

LIVE IT OUT

You're going to be caught off guard this week; how will you respond? Here are some ways to be distinct in your reactions:

▶ **Keep your word.** What is one commitment you've made that you wish you hadn't? Recommit yourself to keeping your word even though it's going to hurt.

▶ **Pray.** Is one relationship particularly difficult for you right now? Pray and ask God to bless that person this week. Even better, write a note and let the person know you've been praying for him or her.

▶ **Go the extra mile.** Think back over the past month. Have you missed any opportunities to do good for someone, an occasion when you chose to do the minimum? Go back and do something extra for that person this week.

Life is about reactions. Things will happen this week you have absolutely no control over, no matter how well you plan. The question is: what happens next? Will you practice grace and integrity when others make demands of you? Or will you hold tightly to your rights and privileges?

My thoughts

I shall plan to seek rightful reparing God B, but I will trust God & accept the "injustice" if I have to, with God's help. OR, it is easy to pray for them, & let go of what is lost because it was always God's anyway.

SESSION 6
DISTINCT IN MY LOVE

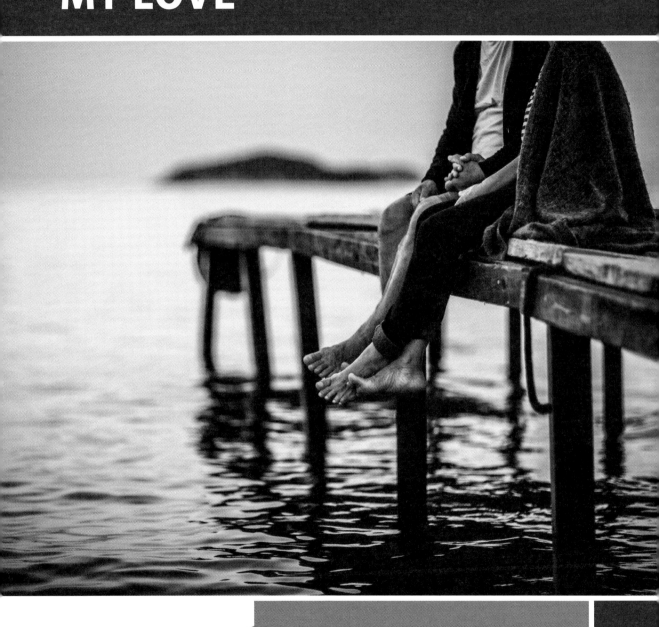

When is it appropriate
to use the word "love"?

QUESTION #1

#BSFLdistinct

BIBLE STUDIES FOR LIFE **47**

Love everyone unconditionally.

THE BIBLE MEETS LIFE

In America today, we "love" *everything*. Think about all the ways you use that four-letter word during a given week. We love burgers, children, puppies, ice cream, college football, spring days, vacations, action movies, romantic movies, and gazillions of other things.

Isn't it amazing that, with the wealth of words we have at our disposal in the English language, we use the same term to describe our feelings about a hot dog as we do to describe our relationship with our mothers? Surely we can't feel the same way about a cat video on the Internet as we do about our own children.

Most of the time, we use the word "love" to describe anything that makes us feel good at a given moment. With that definition, it's no wonder we fall out of love with people at about the same rate we fall out of love with certain kinds of food.

Jesus calls us to something more. As His followers, we are called to love in the way He does. That standard of love is unconditional and knows no limits. Now that's distinct!

WHAT DOES THE BIBLE SAY?

Matthew 5:43-48

43 "You have heard that it was said, Love your neighbor and hate your enemy.

44 But I tell you, love your enemies and pray for those who persecute you,

45 so that you may be sons of your Father in heaven. For He causes His sun to rise on the evil and the good, and sends rain on the righteous and the unrighteous.

46 For if you love those who love you, what reward will you have? Don't even the tax collectors do the same?

47 And if you greet only your brothers, what are you doing out of the ordinary? Don't even the Gentiles do the same?

48 Be perfect, therefore, as your heavenly Father is perfect."

Perfect (v. 48)—The term can mean flawless. It can also have the sense of mature, complete, or fully developed in a moral or spiritual sense. In reference to God's people, "mature" or "complete" is the more likely meaning.

Matthew 5:43-45

Most of the world operates by a simple premise: Love those who love you. In this worldview, people only get into relationships for what they can gain from them. Every relationship is self-serving; thus, if a relationship ceases to give you what you want, you simply move onto the next one.

The kingdom of God does not operate that way.

Jesus called us to love those who feel animosity and even hatred toward us. He gave us an example from weather: when the rain falls, the evil receive the benefit in the same way the righteous do. This is God's "common grace." It's "common" because He extends it to everyone. This doesn't mean God approves of everything that happens on the earth. It only means God's love is completely distinct from our love. He extends His love to people not because they love Him, but because it's in His character to do so.

Jesus gave us our marching orders: love and pray. And don't just pray for people who wish you good; also pray for those who wish you evil.

> **What are some practical ways to love those we don't like?**
>
> QUESTION #2

- ▶ **Prayer shapes our hearts.** When we pray for someone who is difficult to love, we will find our hearts being bent *toward* that person. The reason is simple: it's hard to hate someone you are asking God to bless and help.

- ▶ **Prayer expresses our love.** Prayer is one of the best ways we have to express our love for someone. We are asking the God of the universe to exercise His power on behalf of someone else, for his or her good. That's powerful!

> **When has prayer changed your attitude and actions toward someone difficult to love?**
>
> QUESTION #3

[handwritten notes: Prayers. And allowing returning good for evil. Give them what they need. Show mercy.]

[handwritten notes: can't remember. But I decide to, because God requires it. + I have prayer for grace to love.]

Matthew 5:46-47

If we only love those who love us in return, that's easy. Tax collectors were locals who had gone over to the side of the Romans because of their own greed. They collected taxes for Rome, plus whatever additional money they deemed fit. Needless to say, the tax collectors were despised. But even they loved those who loved them.

Similarly, the Jews looked down on the Gentiles as irreligious people, pagan in both nature and customs. Gentiles didn't have the first idea about who God is, and their actions showed it. But Jesus maintained that even the Gentiles greeted those they called brothers.

Jesus was not validating the contempt that flowed through the community toward the tax collectors and Gentiles. Instead, He was using the people's own self-righteousness and judgment against them. Even the tax collectors and Gentiles loved in the easy way.

Jesus calls His followers to a harder kind of love. He wants us to put ourselves out there, risk rejection and ridicule, and then do it all over again—with no thought of reciprocation.

According to Jesus, the defining mark of His true follower is love. Love is the one element of discipleship that can't be faked. Many people might perform miracles and do all kinds of other religious deeds, but that doesn't mean they will enter the kingdom of heaven (see Matt. 7:22-23). We can become very adept at "playing disciple" by sheer acts of will. But you can't manufacture genuine love.

Jesus said, "By this all people will know that you are My disciples, if you have love for one another" (John 13:35). Let me say it again: love is the greatest defining mark of a Christian. Those who truly love demonstrate they have experienced the love of Jesus Christ and are growing in their understanding of the great love of God in Christ.

> **What do we risk when we embrace Jesus' definition of love?**

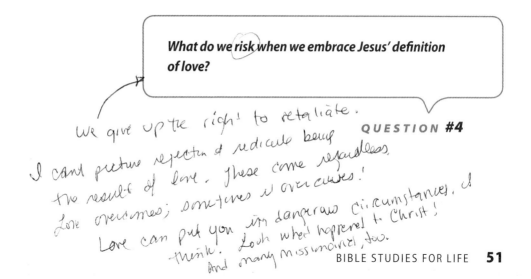

We give up the right to retaliate.

I can't picture rejection & ridicule being the result of love. These come regardless. Love overcomes; sometimes it overcomes!

Love can put you in dangerous circumstances. I think. Look what happened to Christ! And many missionaries, too.

QUESTION #4

Matthew 5:48

When we see the word *perfect*, we tend to think of something flawless. Without error. Pristine. If that's what Jesus meant in verse 48, it becomes an absolutely crushing statement.

Thankfully, that's not the case. Jesus didn't have that kind of perfection in mind. The word He used here wasn't so much about flawlessness, but function.

Imagine you're a young parent preparing to assemble a crib. You open the box and see a dizzying array of diagrams and parts. As you assemble the crib, you notice a set of screws that require a special tool to tighten them. Fortunately, the manufacturer included a tool that fits just right; the bed finally comes together. That tool was the *perfect* tool for its function. You might never use it again, but for that moment, and on that particular occasion, it fit just right. Was the tool absolutely perfect, in terms of its flawlessness? Probably not. But to do the job it was designed for, it was good and right. It was *perfect*.

We need to look at Jesus' call to be perfect in terms of our function. Verse 48 reminds us that we are distinct among God's creation. We were created in His image to relate to Him in a unique way.

To be created in God's image means we were made to display God's character and glory in every part of our lives. We should strive to be the kind of parent God is. And we should love like God does:

▶ God loves those who don't acknowledge Him.

▶ God is generous to those who don't recognize or reciprocate His generosity.

▶ God provides for those who are ungrateful.

▶ And we are to be like Him.

That's what makes us distinct.

> **What are some opportunities we have to express unconditional love?**
>
> QUESTION **#5**

[handwritten notes:] manuali ~~manuali~~ donations! Love those on the other side of the political divide - pray for them. ?

BE PERFECT?

Your relationships	*Your finances*

No resentment regarding
others costing me.
give more & spend less on me.

Your emotions	*Your dreams*

How have you been blessed in these categories through your relationship with God?

- Overcome problems with Susen (Sister).
- generousity - much more so because of God
- helped me set aside my dreams to serve my family
- Overcame much negative emotions by looking at difficulties through eyes of faith.

LIVE IT OUT

Showing love the way God loves is what makes us truly distinct. Let's look for opportunities to stand apart from the rest of the world.

▶ **Pray.** Commit to pray every day for one person in your life who is difficult to love. Pray that God would bless that person. Notice how your heart softens toward that person.

▶ **Thank.** Have you ever been difficult to love? Think of someone who loved you during a time when you were hard to love. Make a call and express your thanks for the way his or her love reminded you of the way God loves all the time.

▶ **Sacrifice.** Jesus loves us sacrificially. What is one practical way you can sacrificially love someone else this week?

It's OK to love ice cream. And puppies. And college football. But don't confuse all that love with God's love—the love He calls you to walk in. God loves you. Now go and do likewise.

My thoughts

A TIME FOR GOD

BY PHILIP NATION

"If only ..." is how I've started so many sentences in my life. After all, I'm human and it is our nature to crave more. We constantly strain for meaning in the everyday grind of life. It is the search for margin so that we can take a breath, grab a moment to rest, and find some peace. The "if onlys" are the desperate longing for God to make His presence abundantly clear in the ordinary parts of life.

If only that could happen.

Living an "If Only" Life

I'm a believer who works hard all week in two jobs that normally equal 65-75 hours a week. I'm a husband who wants to provide better for my wife and not be a knucklehead in our relationship. I'm a parent to two teenage sons and would like to not mess up their launch into manhood. If only I could do better by them, then life would be at least OK. But I'm busy with so much on the periphery of my core relationships that I feel sucked into vortexes of busyness that hamper everything of importance.

Often, my "if only" statements come because I'm greedy and arrogant. Go ahead, admit that it happens to you, too. It's good for the soul. It is often the exclamation that I deserve more. If only life were fair to me. If only I got the promotion instead of [insert name of your nemesis at work]. If only I had more. But the demands we make on life are simply short-sighted. More now might be distracting. The job you think you want today might be a detour to the plan God has for your future. And that is the painful reality of most "if only" statements — they are distractions from what your life truly needs.

Learning from The Teacher

The Teacher is the central character of Ecclesiastes. It is the book that is often in the clean, white pages of our Bibles where the gilded edges are still stuck together. But, we need it today more than ever. It gives us the story of a man (who, if not King Solomon, portrays himself as such) has everything in life until he realizes he is horribly mistaken.

Ecclesiastes is filled with an ancient set of "if only" circumstances. The Teacher has plenty enough power, money, pleasure, and knowledge to last several lifetimes. But he wants more, only to discover that the "more" he craved actually left him dissatisfied. Throughout the book, we get the phrases of: "Vanity of vanities, saith the Preacher, vanity of vanities; all is vanity" (KJV). "Meaningless! Meaningless!" says the Teacher. "Utterly meaningless! Everything is meaningless" (NIV). "Absolute futility," says the Teacher. "Absolute futility. Everything is futile" (HCSB).

"Absolute futility," says the Teacher.
"Absolute futility. Everything is futile."

—ECCLESIASTES 1:2 (HCSB)

It is the signal that we need to look at life through a new lens. The things we lay our hands on, try to seize and hold onto—it's all temporary. They are here for a moment and then gone. The impulse dovetails into The Teacher's reminder that there is nothing new under the sun. Everything that we see today has happened before and will happen again (see Ecclesiastes 1:9-10). In other words, everything is on repeat. The human experience is cyclical. All of the curiosities that we invent to entertain, explore, and bide our time—it is just a version of what others have done and will do.

Entering the Silence

Ecclesiastes is an ancient answer to our modern lives. As the Teacher moves from issue to issue, it all seems so similar. He is describing the rat-race we all face. The culture is different, but the circumstances are not. We fight to get ahead financially. We position our kids to be the most popular, most athletic, Valedictorian-like pupils possible. We look for peace but, like the Teacher, we find futility. In the end, the solution is quite simple. We are looking for eternal among the temporary. It is why, in the middle of the book, The Teacher does the unexpected. He silently enters the presence of God.

The fifth chapter of Ecclesiastes begins with what seems to be an out-of-place paragraph about how to approach God. Everything preceding it and following it (for the most part) is a commentary on the futility of chasing after any meaning. Then, in what feels a bit like scriptural whiplash, we are thrust into the house of God. But, it is such a necessary redirection. While The Teacher has been chasing the world's solutions, he's only been chasing his tail because there's nothing new under the sun. What he needs — and what we need — is a dose of reality. The truest reality is the presence of God. So, he reminds us that when you approach God, do it silently.

Why the need for silence? It is not for just a mental health break. It is not because we live in an ocean of noise with the oh-so-occasional respite of quiet. It is because we should not dare to bargain with God for what we want. The only true solutions to life's mysteries of enjoyment, acquiring necessities, and gaining wisdom are found when we are silent before the Lord.

The point that he makes, and that we need to hear, is that the best route to take in the presence of God is silent obedience and loving awe. When we rush into prayer, worship, devotions, or any religious activity, we are tempted to do so thinking that we are the main attraction. We think God must be so pleased that I showed up to pray to Him today. Not even close. If we get this wrong, we get it all wrong. The hasty list of wants and the half-hearted devotion toward obedience will cause us to write a check that our account can't cover. Instead, we enter His presence in loving awe of how God's majesty outshines every toy, hobby, and accomplishment in this life.

Discovering the Answer

Interestingly, when we couple the need for silence before God and living in worshipful adoration of Him ("fear the Lord"), then we can actually enjoy life. By the way, it is much of what Ecclesiastes is about. In the middle of marriage and parenting, work and hobbies, winning and losing at our endeavors — we are searching for how all that is temporary connects with the eternal. We want a resolution to the eternity that is in our hearts (see 3:11). Coming face to face with the overwhelming presence of God and being silent while He directs, then we come to the same conclusion as The Teacher: "Fear God and keep His commands, for this is for all humanity" (12:13). The God-shaped vacuum in our hearts, described by Blaise Pascal, is yearning for something that can't be filled by the stuff of earth. The craving that we have attempted to feed through drink and sex and money and entertainment is not satisfied so easily. The fellowship and following of our great Savior, however, will. Fear God and keep His commands — six simple words with the deepest of meanings.

It is a command beautifully set in the landscape of the gospel. Jesus completely sets our relationship status right before Himself so we can find enjoyment in the very issues over which The Teacher struggled. In Christ, work is set in its proper place and we can enjoy the accomplishments that occur. Pleasure is seen in a new light of foreshadowing eternal glories. All of our relationships become people to nurture rather than pawns to control. We can enjoy people and have our appetites whetted for knowing God and fellow believers forever. All the things that we used to chase after are now signposts for higher realities.

Now, whenever I bump against the abrasive parts of life, my "if only" is stated with a longing for the eternal. I know that life will brutalize me, but it is all a temporary setback because of Christ's wounds that have brought me healing. Every task at work, diaper changed, teenager launched into quasi-adulthood, fender-bender survived, and relationship navigated with some level of success is a signal of greater things yet to come. Today, when I stare into the Word or into the world, I think of heaven and know that there is a great fulfilling moment arriving soon for my "if only."

This article has been excerpted from HomeLife *magazine.*

—Philip Nation is a publishing director for LifeWay and teaching pastor for The Fellowship in Nashville, Tenn. He has authored numerous books and Bible studies including *Compelled: Living the Mission of God* and *Storm Shelter: Encountering God in the Psalms.* Philip and his wife Angie have two sons, Andrew and Chris. Find out more about him at *philipnation.net.*

My group's prayer requests

....

....

....

....

....

....

....

....

....

....

....

My thoughts

LEADER GUIDE | DISTINCT

GENERAL INSTRUCTIONS

In order to make the most of this study and to ensure a richer group experience, it's recommended that all group participants read through the teaching and discussion content in full before each group meeting. As a leader, it is also a good idea for you to be familiar with this content and prepared to summarize it for your group members as you move through the material each week.

Each session of the Bible study is made up of three sections:

1. THE BIBLE MEETS LIFE.

An introduction to the theme of the session and its connection to everyday life, along with a brief overview of the primary Scripture text. This section also includes an icebreaker question or activity.

2. WHAT DOES THE BIBLE SAY?

This comprises the bulk of each session and includes the primary Scripture text along with explanations for key words and ideas within that text. This section also includes most of the content designed to produce and maintain discussion within the group.

3. LIVE IT OUT.

The final section focuses on application, using bulleted summary statements to answer the question, *So what?* As the leader, be prepared to challenge the group to apply what they learned during the discussion by transforming it into action throughout the week.

For group leaders, the *Distinct* Leader Guide contains several features and tools designed to help you lead participants through the material provided.

QUESTION 1—ICEBREAKER

These opening questions and/or activities are designed to help participants transition into the study and begin engaging the primary themes to be discussed. Be sure everyone has a chance to speak, but maintain a low-pressure environment.

DISCUSSION QUESTIONS

Each "What Does the Bible Say?" section features six questions designed to spark discussion and interaction within your group. These questions encourage critical thinking, so be sure to allow a period of silence for participants to process the question and form an answer.

The *Distinct* Leader Guide also contains follow-up questions and optional activities that may be helpful to your group, if time permits.

DVD CONTENT

Each video features Michael Kelley discussing the primary themes found in the session. We recommend you show this video in one of three places: (1) At the beginning of the group time, (2) After the icebreaker, or (3) After a quick review and/or summary of "What Does the Bible Say?" A video summary is included as well. You may choose to use this summary as background preparation to help you guide the group.

The Leader Guide contains additional questions to help unpack the video and transition into the discussion. For a digital Leader Guide with commentary, see the "Leader Tools" folder on the DVD-ROM in your Leader Kit.

For helps on how to use *Bible Studies for Life,* tips on how to better lead groups, or additional ideas for leading, visit: *ministrygrid.com/web/BibleStudiesforLife.*

The Point: Choose actions and attitudes that are blessed by God.

The Passage: Matthew 5:1-12

The Setting: Early in His earthly ministry, Jesus gathered His disciples around Him and began to teach them the differences between commonly accepted religious truths and the fuller truth from God's perspective. Though He taught His disciples, crowds gathered around to hear Him teach. He began with what we call the Beatitudes, a series of blessings on people most would not have considered blessed.

QUESTION 1: What was the happiest time in your life?

> *Optional activity:* Supplement "The Bible Meets Life" by playing several popular commercials on a laptop or tablet—or by instructing group members to search for and play specific commercials using their phones. As you watch each commercial, encourage group members to consider the following questions: 1) What product is being sold? 2) How does the commercial connect this product to your desire for happiness?

> *Note:* Be sure to select commercials that are appropriate for the members of your specific group. Lean toward commercials that are humorous rather than commercials focused on sexuality or exploitation.

Video Summary: Jesus is calling us to live a life that stands out, that is distinct. Yet many of us grow up fearing that very thing—that we will stand out. There is a desire in us to fit in, to be just like everyone else. But God's desire for us isn't that we would blend it. He desires that we live differently. As believers, when we live truly distinct lives, our character reflects our identity in Christ.

▶ WATCH THE DVD SEGMENT FOR SESSION 1. THEN USE THE FOLLOWING QUESTIONS AND DISCUSSION POINTS TO TRANSITION INTO THE STUDY.

  ● Think of how you typically use the word *blessed* in normal conversation. How has your definition differed from that of Matthew 5:1-12?

  ● In what ways do you believe others would say your "fruit displays your root"?

WHAT DOES THE BIBLE SAY?

▶ ASK FOR A VOLUNTEER TO READ ALOUD MATTHEW 5:1-12.

Response: What's your initial reaction to these verses?

  ● What do you like about the text?

  ● What questions do you have about these verses?

▶ TURN THE GROUP'S ATTENTION TO MATTHEW 5:1-6.

QUESTION 2: What is your understanding of what it means to be blessed?

This question requires that group members interpret this passage for themselves as a way to move toward life application. Encourage them to also examine their own definition beside that of Matthew 5:1-6. If you took part in the video discussion, you may have started this conversation there.

> *Optional follow-up:* What do Jesus' teachings in this passage reveal about the kingdom of God?

▶ MOVE TO MATTHEW 5:7-9.

QUESTION 3: When have you felt the cost of choosing to show mercy, be pure, or make peace?

This question will allow group members an opportunity to share personal stories as well as acknowledge and reflect on how their lives have been affected by choosing to live in sharp distinction to the world.

> *Optional activity:* Direct group members to complete the activity "Feeling Blessed" on page 11. If time permits, encourage volunteers to share some of the major blessings in their lives.

> *Optional follow-up:* Which of the attributes in these verses do you find easiest to live out?

▶ CONTINUE WITH MATTHEW 5:10-12.

QUESTION 4: What are some ways Christians experience persecution in today's world?

Direct group member to consider examples from their day to day experiences as well as stories we hear through the media. This question will help group members consider obstacles that can distract us from living in a way that is counterintuitive to what society expects.

> *Optional follow-up:* What are some ways you have experienced persecution on a personal level?

QUESTION 5: How do we help one another choose joy when others mistreat us because of our faith?

This is an application question included to encourage group members to create steps they will take as a group to act on the biblical principles presented in this session.

> *Optional follow-up:* What are some ways you have seen others choose joy that have inspired you to do the same?

Note: The following question does not appear in the group member book. Use it in your group discussion as time allows.

QUESTION 6: How have you experienced a blessing after choosing to go against the flow?

Sharing and storytelling represent great ways for growing as a group. This question creates an environment for sharing relative to the text.

LIVE IT OUT

Encourage group members to consider the following ways they can seek out blessing rather than mere happiness:

- **Allow God's Word to bless you.** Memorize Matthew 5:3-6 and pray through Jesus' words every day.

- **Bless someone else by serving them.** Choose one relationship this week in which you want to model what it means to be blessed. Serve that person in a tangible way.

- **Allow someone else to bless you.** Share with someone you trust about a tough situation you are walking through. Ask him or her to help you choose to be glad and rejoice in the middle of that situation.

Challenge: Christians are different; they are distinct. They display that distinction in their dependence on God, their actions toward others, and the way they respond to difficulties. Spend some time this week watching other Christians, maybe at church or in your small group. Pay attention to the ways they bless others through their actions.

Pray: Ask for prayer requests and ask group members to pray for the different requests as intercessors. As the leader, close this time by asking the Lord to help each of you remember to seek God's blessings rather than happiness. Conclude by verbally submitting yourself to the principles Jesus taught in the Beatitudes. Confess your desire to live distinctly as a member of God's kingdom in this world.

SESSION 2: DISTINCT IN MY INFLUENCE

The Point: Make your influence count for what matters.

The Passage: Matthew 5:13-20

The Setting: As Jesus taught His disciples directly, and the crowds less directly, He addressed a variety of subjects. In the passage for this session, He highlighted the responsibility of His followers toward the broader society, namely to be salt and light. He also addressed accusations (because He didn't heed the misguided religious interpretations and implications of past generations) that He broke God's law, perhaps even seeking to destroy it.

QUESTION 1: What flavoring or spice could you not live without?

> *Optional activity:* Supplement Question 1 by bringing a number of common spices and flavorings to the group gathering. Bring what you have in your home or purchase a few of the more popular options—hot sauce, cinnamon, curry, mustard, salsa, and so on. Encourage group members to pass items around the group and discuss which they like best with different foods.

> *Note:* If you really want to make a splash, consider bringing plain crackers and chips and allowing group members to sample the different spices and flavorings for themselves.

Video Summary: Christians aren't meant to simply be in the mix of the culture or just to stand out in the mix; we're meant to influence the world around us. As Jesus continued the Sermon on the Mount, He gave some illustrations of how this influence happens. He called us to be salt and light. Just because we are *in* the world, doesn't mean we shouldn't use our influence to be distinct *from* the world.

▶ WATCH THE DVD SEGMENT FOR SESSION 2. THEN USE THE FOLLOWING QUESTIONS AND DISCUSSION POINTS TO TRANSITION INTO THE STUDY.

- Consider what a normal day looks like for you. What are some ways you can be *in* the world but not *of* it?

- In what ways might you better prepare yourself for the opportunities God has built into your daily schedule for you to be a distinct influence? Be specific.

WHAT DOES THE BIBLE SAY?

▶ ASK FOR A VOLUNTEER TO READ ALOUD MATTHEW 5:13-20.

Response: What's your initial reaction to these verses?

- What questions do you have about these verses?

- What do you hope to learn this week about how you can truly make a difference with your influence?

▶ TURN THE GROUP'S ATTENTION TO MATTHEW 5:13.

QUESTION 2: Salt flavors and preserves. How do Christians both preserve and improve culture?

This question is designed to give group members an opportunity to consider the impact they can have on culture by retaining their uniqueness as His people while influencing those around them.

Optional follow-up: What are some specific ways God uses us to make people thirsty for Him?

▶ MOVE TO MATTHEW 5:14-16.

QUESTION 3: How do we shine our light in a way that brings glory to God and not ourselves?

This question is designed to help group members actively engage the Scripture text and then interpret, in their own words, what life application of this passage looks like.

Optional activity: Direct group members to complete the activity "Light of the World" on page 19. If time permits, encourage volunteers to share their responses.

▶ CONTINUE WITH MATTHEW 5:17-20.

QUESTION 4: When has the Bible sparked your ability to live as salt and light?

This question invites members of the group to share their personal testimonies of ways they have been able to apply the scriptural text to their daily lives.

Optional follow-up: What are some key disciplines that help you obey God's Word?

QUESTION 5: What's one step you can take this week to live as salt and light in your community?

Your goal for this question is to help group members think through practical ideas for how they can live distinct in their influence. Encourage them to be specific in their responses and to push beyond the most obvious answers.

Note: The following question does not appear in the group member book. Use it in your group discussion as time allows.

QUESTION 6: What hinders believers from fulfilling their distinct purposes as salt and light?

This question is designed to help group members consider hindrances that can get in the way of fulfilling their distinct purposes. Answers will vary based on their individual experiences.

Optional follow-up: In what ways can being aware of these hindrances better prepare you when you encounter them?

LIVE IT OUT

Invite group members to consider the following suggestions for how they can serve as salt and light in their world this week:

- **Pray for the darkness.** Christians often complain about the darkness in our world—but that accomplishes nothing. Instead, commit to praying each day when you encounter elements of society that need to experience the salt and light of Christ.

- **Don't go it alone.** Identify a believer in Christ whom you respect—someone who uses his or her influence in a positive way. Ask to meet with that person to help you follow Jesus more closely.

- **Speak up.** Look for a chance this week to speak directly about the gospel at a place outside your church or Bible study group.

Challenge: We're all mixed together in this world, which means everyone has the chance to influence everyone else. The question is how we'll use the opportunities we've been given. What opportunities might you have missed to be salt and light? How can you protect yourself from outside influences that might distract you from impacting others in a positive way?

Pray: Ask for prayer requests and ask group members to pray for the different requests as intercessors. As the leader, conclude by praising God for granting you, and the members of your group, opportunities to serve as salt and light in your community. Ask for wisdom and direction as you seek to take advantage of those opportunities this week.

SESSION 3: DISTINCT IN MY APPROACH TO CONFLICT

The Point: Take the lead in resolving conflict.

The Passage: Matthew 5:21-26

The Setting: Having just related that He had not come to destroy God's law but to fulfill it (vv. 17-20), Jesus then began to give examples of what He meant. He did this by taking several of the Ten Commandments and another highly regarded command and stressing the shortcoming of popular interpretations by emphasizing the fuller intent behind them. The subject of this session is the Sixth Commandment, "Do not murder."

QUESTION 1: When have you regretted settling for a quick fix?

> *Optional activity:* Give group members a challenge as a transition between Question 1 and "The Bible Meets Life." Prior to the group gathering, use scissors to make a small cut in several uninflated balloons—enough for each person in your group. You will also need a box of Band-Aids®. During the group gathering, give each person a balloon, along with a Band-Aid. Challenge everyone to fix the cut in the balloon well enough to inflate it and have it retain air.

> *Note:* If your group is especially competitive, turn this activity into a race by awarding a small prize to the first person who can inflate his or her balloon.

Video Summary: As Jesus continued to teach through His Sermon on the Mount, He came to the subject of anger. But anger isn't just a surface issue. Anger is a matter of the heart. While some people run from anger and conflict, others seem to embrace it. Jesus offers an approach to conflict that is distinct from what we see in the world around us. We don't need to hide from conflict, but we can appropriately and lovingly work toward reconciliation. When we choose to make peace, we start to look more like our Father in heaven.

▶ WATCH THE DVD SEGMENT FOR SESSION 3. THEN USE THE FOLLOWING QUESTIONS AND DISCUSSION POINTS TO TRANSITION INTO THE STUDY.

- What situation in your life is calling for you to be a peacemaker and take the first step toward resolving conflict?
- How can you begin that process? Be specific.

WHAT DOES THE BIBLE SAY?

▶ ASK FOR A VOLUNTEER TO READ ALOUD MATTHEW 5:21-26.

Response: What's your initial reaction to these verses?

- What questions do you have about these verses?
- What new application do you hope to get from this passage?

▶ TURN THE GROUP'S ATTENTION TO MATTHEW 5:21-22

QUESTION 2: What's your initial reaction to verses 21-22?

This question requires group members to closely examine the biblical text before answering based on how the passage personally impacted them. As time allows, encourage them to explain their responses.

> *Optional follow-up:* Why do you react to these verses in this way? What are the roots of your reactions?

> *Optional follow-up:* How do we know if our anger is acceptable or unacceptable?

▶ MOVE TO MATTHEW 5:23-24.

QUESTION 3: Reconciliation requires honesty, humility, and security. Which of these do you find challenging?

Use this question as an opportunity to remind group members that there are no "correct" answers for most discussion questions. You're asking for their personal thoughts and ideas.

> *Optional follow-up:* How do we apply these verses to our modern experiences with worship?

> *Optional activity:* Direct group members to complete the activity "Personal Assessment: Anger" on page 27.

▶ CONTINUE WITH MATTHEW 5:25-26.

QUESTION 4: What are some concrete principles Jesus established in this passage?

This question requires group members to closely examine the Scripture passage in order to accurately respond.

> *Optional follow-up:* How would you summarize Jesus' teachings in these verses?

QUESTION 5: What are the consequences of allowing a conflict to fester?

Encourage group members to think about the consequences from several different perspectives—consequences for you, for the person you're in conflict with, for the larger community, and so on.

Note: The following question does not appear in the group member book. Use it in your group discussion as time allows.

QUESTION 6: What steps would we take to successfully resolve any conflicts in this group?

This question is associated with building biblical community. Developing an action plan as a group creates connection and accountability among the members. Belonging to redemptive community is an important aspect of living distinct lives for Christ.

> *Optional follow-up:* What steps do you need to take as an individual to help your group successfully resolve conflict?

LIVE IT OUT

Anger is an issue of the heart. Encourage group members to consider the following suggestions for how they can bring their anger under the rule of Jesus in the days to come:

- **Take control of your anger.** You know what situations are likely to make you angry this week. Prepare your heart and mind to respond appropriately before you ever step into that situation.

- **Say you're sorry.** Look for a chance to say "I'm sorry" this week without qualification. Humble yourself before Christ and the other person, and say those two words that can bring healing.

- **Seek reconciliation.** Examine your relationships, past and present. Is there someone you still need to reconcile with? If so, don't wait any longer. Seek to honor Christ through the process of reconciliation.

Challenge: Spend time this week studying more of what God's Word has to say about handling anger. Focus on passages such as James 1:20; Romans 12; Galatians 6:1-10; 2 Corinthians 1:3-5; Hebrews 3:13; Romans 12:1-2; Galatians 5:23.

Pray: Ask for prayer requests and ask group members to pray for the different requests as intercessors. As the leader, close this time by acknowledging that conflict is a part of life, but as Christians we are called to look deeper into the cause of our anger and seek healing.

SESSION 4: DISTINCT IN MY RELATIONSHIPS

The Point: Hold on to purity at all costs.

The Passage: Matthew 5:27-32

The Setting: The passage for this session addresses the Seventh Commandment, "Do not commit adultery." As with so much of the direction God had given His people over the years, efforts had been made to limit the scope of God's intention, focusing on outward actions only. As Jesus spoke of adultery, and its corollary divorce, He held up the exalted view of marriage that God had set forth for His people.

QUESTION 1: When was the last time you couldn't hear yourself think?

> *Optional activity:* Transition between Question 1 and "The Bible Meets Life" by encouraging group members to spend 30 seconds in complete silence. Instruct everyone to put down their books, phones, and so on. Ask them to close their eyes and simply listen to the silence for half a minute.

> *Note:* When finished, be sure to ask group members how they felt during this "moment of silence." Encourage them to share what they were thinking and what emotions they experienced.

Video Summary: Faithfulness and purity have been a wonder to our culture, but it should be our norm. Purity is a battle that is waged in our hearts. Jesus calls us to sexual purity, both physically and mentally. It's not just a call to purity in terms of our actions, but in our very being. It's a call for absolute agreement in our thoughts, feelings, and actions. Ultimately, temptation is not about our ability to say no. It's about what we believe to be true about God.

▶ WATCH THE DVD SEGMENT FOR SESSION 4. THEN USE THE FOLLOWING QUESTIONS AND DISCUSSION POINTS TO TRANSITION INTO THE STUDY.

> ● Michael says, "Ultimately, temptation is not about your ability to say no. It's about what you believe to be true about God. … Do you believe that God really loves you or do you believe He is holding something back from you?" Spend some time talking as a group about how what you believe to be true about the character of God impacts your ability to live distinct in your relationships.

WHAT DOES THE BIBLE SAY?

▶ ASK FOR A VOLUNTEER TO READ ALOUD MATTHEW 5:27-32.

Response: What's your initial reaction to these verses?

> ● What do you like about the text?
> ● What new application do you hope to receive about God's call to live pure lives?

▶ TURN THE GROUP'S ATTENTION TO MATTHEW 5:27-30.

QUESTION 2: What are the dividing lines between "pure" and "impure" in today's world?

The goal here is to help group members consider how modern culture defines and influences our beliefs and actions related to purity.

> ***Optional follow-up:*** What are the dividing lines between "pure" and "impure" in Scripture?

QUESTION 3: How can we be ruthless in resisting impurity without being judgmental and condemning?

The goal here is to help group members consider how modern culture has influenced our beliefs about relationships and how we can live in a way that is so distinct that others take notice.

▶ MOVE TO MATTHEW 5:31-32.

QUESTION 4: Whom do you look to as a model of faithfulness?

This question will allow group members an opportunity to share personal stories as well as acknowledge and reflect on how others have impacted their view of what true faithfulness looks like.

> ***Optional activity:*** Direct group members to complete the activity "Seeking Sources" on page 35. (Note: You may also consider asking group members to complete this activity in private.)

QUESTION 5: How do we love God and love others in a culture of divorce?

The goal of this question is to address how we communicate and support a biblical standard for marriage without alienating those inside and outside the church who have personal experience with divorce.

> ***Optional follow-up:*** How do we demonstrate a positive example of purity in today's culture?

Note: The following question does not appear in the group member book. Use it in your group discussion as time allows.

QUESTION 6: What are some keys to maintaining faithfulness in marriage over the long haul?

This question requires that group members interpret this Scripture passage for themselves as a way to move them toward life application.

> ***Optional follow-up:*** What steps can you take to intentionally pursue faithfulness in your relationships?

LIVE IT OUT

Holding on to purity isn't always easy, but it's always valuable. Invite group members to consider the following suggestions for ways they can seek purity this week:

- **Replace.** What is one way you are spending your time that is not contributing to your personal purity? Look for something to replace it this week.

- **Serve.** Consider a practical way you can serve your spouse this week. For example, intentionally do the one thing around the house your spouse doesn't enjoy doing.

- **Talk.** Begin the process of accountability by letting your guard down with someone you trust. Initiate a conversation with that person and share one way in which you are struggling to hold on to purity at all costs.

Challenge: You don't have to settle for the world's standard of purity and faithfulness. God has something more. If you're holding onto mistakes you've made in the past, ask the Lord to reveal those to you. Ask His forgiveness if you haven't already done so; consider journaling about any emotions you're experiencing; and ask Him to help you move on, seeking purity in your relationships.

Pray: Ask for prayer requests and ask group members to pray for the different requests as intercessors. As the leader, close this time by asking the Lord to quiet the "noise" that keeps you from hearing His truth and to instead seek out the life of purity He calls us to live. Conclude by expressing your desire to strive for purity at all costs, both as individuals and as a group. Also express your willingness to serve as examples for God's standard of purity in an impure culture.

SESSION 5: DISTINCT IN MY REACTIONS

The Point: Practice grace and integrity when others make demands of you.

The Passage: Matthew 5:33-42

The Setting: Jesus did not quote or directly reference one of the Ten Commandments in the passage for this session, but He did address the essence of the Ninth Commandment, "Do not give false testimony against your neighbor." While the Commandment specifically focuses on one's legal or moral witness in regard to another, its heart is the need for God's people to display integrity with their words. Jesus raised the need for integrity in one's words (see vv. 33-37) and in one's approach to others (see vv. 38-42).

QUESTION 1: When have you felt like you were organized and on top of things?

> *Optional activity:* Supplement "The Bible Meets Life" by providing some real-life interruptions for members of your group. Prior to the group gathering, seek out the phone numbers of several people in your group. Program those numbers into your phone. Then, while the group discusses Question 1, place several calls to group members physically present in the room with you. The goal is to get their phones to ring, causing interruptions.

> *Note:* If you don't want to make phone calls during the discussion, you could ask a friend or family member outside the group to make the calls for you at a predetermined time.

Video Summary: Life is about reaction. Everything said or done to us will cause us to react, but how we react is totally in our hands. Our reactions are an opportunity for us to be distinct. The way we react will—or won't—show us to be distinctly Christian. Jesus calls us to live lives of integrity—people who are the same in public and in private. People who make commitments and keep them. Jesus calls us to a standard that is consistent, honest, and filled with grace.

▶ WATCH THE DVD SEGMENT FOR SESSION 5. THEN USE THE FOLLOWING QUESTIONS AND DISCUSSION POINTS TO TRANSITION INTO THE STUDY.

- In what situations do you find it easy to be generous? Explain.
- In what situations do you find it difficult to be generous? Explain.

WHAT DOES THE BIBLE SAY?

▶ ASK FOR A VOLUNTEER TO READ ALOUD MATTHEW 5:33-42.

Response: What's your initial reaction to these verses?

- What questions do you have about these verses?
- What new application do you hope to get from this passage?

▶ TURN THE GROUP'S ATTENTION TO MATTHEW 5:33-37.

QUESTION 2: What motivates us to say, "I promise"?

This question is designed to help group members consider circumstances that lead them to make promises. Encourage them to examine their motivations in those situations.

Optional follow-up: Why are we often quick to make promises we're not certain we can keep?

▶ MOVE TO MATTHEW 5:38-39.

QUESTION 3: What are some practical ways to turn the other cheek in today's culture?

This question requires group members to interpret this Scripture passage and then determine how it can be applied to their daily lives. Encourage them to consider specific situations in their own lives as they answer.

Optional follow-up: When have you admired someone who turned the other cheek?

QUESTION 4: When do we cross the line between turning the other cheek and living as a victim?

You may want to approach this question by discussing the motivations and consequences of making the choice not to turn the other cheek. Also spend some time talking about things that indicate we have crossed this line.

▶ CONTINUE WITH MATTHEW 5:40-42.

QUESTION 5: How do we prepare ourselves now to respond well when others make demands of us?

This is an application question included to encourage group members to create a plan to ensure they are prepared for action. It promotes accountability and the need to act on biblical principles.

Optional follow-up: What keeps us from taking these commands more seriously?

Optional activity: Direct group members to complete the activity "What Would You Say?" on page 45. If time permits, encourage volunteers to share their responses.

Note: The following question does not appear in the group member book. Use it in your group discussion as time allows.

QUESTION 6: What are some specific obstacles that hinder you from demonstrating more grace and integrity in your reactions to others?

Sharing stories is a great way to grow as a group. This question creates an environment for sharing based on the personal experiences of group members.

Optional follow-up: What actions can you take this week to remove these obstacles? Be specific.

LIVE IT OUT

We're going to be caught off guard this week; how will we respond? Encourage group members to consider the following suggestions for ways they can be distinct in their reactions:

- **Keep your word.** What is one commitment you've made that you wish you hadn't? Recommit yourself to keeping your word even though it's going to hurt.

- **Pray.** Is one relationship particularly difficult for you right now? Pray and ask God to bless that person this week. Even better, write a note and let the person know you've been praying for him or her.

- **Go the extra mile.** Think back over the past month. Have you missed any opportunities to do good for someone, an occasion when you chose to do the minimum? Go back and do something extra for that person this week.

Challenge: Life is about reactions. Things will happen this week you have absolutely no control over, no matter how well you plan. The question is: Will you practice grace and integrity when others make demands of you? Or will you hold tightly to your rights and privileges? Commit to spending time in prayer every morning this week asking the Lord to equip and prepare you for what your day holds. Ask Him to help you welcome interruptions and reflect Him in your reaction.

Pray: Ask for prayer requests and ask group members to pray for the different requests as intercessors. As the leader, close this time by asking the Lord to give each of you strength and wisdom to react in grace and integrity to the demands and interruptions in your lives.

SESSION 6: DISTINCT IN MY LOVE

The Point: Love everyone unconditionally.

The Passage: Matthew 5:43-48

The Setting: In Jesus' day, the Jewish people in general and the religious leadership in particular were quite clear on who were their neighbors and who were their enemies, and how they should treat each. While the admonition to "love your neighbor" appears in the Old Testament, the conclusion "and hate your enemy" is a mere extrapolation, and not God's design. This session passage finds Jesus setting the record straight that His followers are to love both neighbor and enemy.

QUESTION 1: When is it appropriate to use the word "love"?

Optional activity: Supplement Question 1 by creating a chart with three categories: "Appropriate," "Maybe," and "Not Appropriate." Encourage group members to identify different times when we use the word *love* for something and then to work as a group to assign each one to a category. For example, your group may decide that using *love* in the context of marriage goes in the "Appropriate" category, while using *love* to describe tacos goes in the "Not Appropriate" category. Again, the goal here is to create a fun debate around our use of the word *love* in today's world.

Note: If you don't have a whiteboard or chalkboard to create the categories, consider taping a large piece of paper to the wall.

Video Summary: Think about all the ways we use the word *love* during a given week. We use the same term to describe our feelings about pizza as we do to describe our relationship with our mothers. We use the word *love* to describe anything that makes us feel good at a given moment. But Jesus is calling us to something more. As His followers, we are called to love in the way He does. That standard of love is unconditional and knows no limits. It's distinct. But unless we believe and trust the love that Jesus has for us, we'll never be able to truly love others.

▶ WATCH THE DVD SEGMENT FOR SESSION 6. THEN USE THE FOLLOWING QUESTIONS AND DISCUSSION POINTS TO TRANSITION INTO THE STUDY.

- When have you consistently prayed for someone who was difficult to love and experienced a change of heart as a result?

- In what ways does your belief and trust in the love Jesus has for you better equip you to truly love others?

WHAT DOES THE BIBLE SAY?

▶ ASK FOR A VOLUNTEER TO READ ALOUD MATTHEW 5:43-48.

Response: What's your initial reaction to these verses?

- What questions do you have about what it means to love unconditionally and without limits?
- What new application do you hope to get from this passage?

▶ TURN THE GROUP'S ATTENTION TO MATTHEW 5:43-45.

QUESTION 2: What are some practical ways to love those we don't like?

It's good to remind group members that there's no "automatic switch" for becoming more loving toward others. Instead, this question provides an opportunity to work together as a group to map out a plan for developing into people who are better able to show unconditional love to others.

Optional follow-up: How would you define an enemy in your life?

QUESTION 3: When has prayer changed your attitude and actions toward someone difficult to love?

This question is a bit more personal in nature. It may take group members several moments to decide what they are comfortable sharing. Give them the time they need.

▶ MOVE TO MATTHEW 5:46-47.

QUESTION 4: What do we risk when we embrace Jesus' definition of love?

Encourage group members to consider this question from multiple angles. What do we risk personally? What do we risk from people in our "tribe"? What do we risk from the culture around us?

Optional follow-up: How does Jesus differentiate between easy love and difficult love in this passage?

▶ CONTINUE WITH MATTHEW 5:48.

QUESTION 5: What are some opportunities we have to express unconditional love?

Once again, encourage group members to think about opportunities in multiple areas of life—at home, at work, at church, in the community, and so on. Also ask them to consider opportunities to express unconditional love both as individuals and as a group.

Optional activity: Direct group members to complete the activity "Be Perfect?" on page 53. If time permits, encourage volunteers to share their responses.

Note: The following question does not appear in the group member book. Use it in your group discussion as time allows.

QUESTION 6: How would you describe your role and function as a follower of God?

Ask group members to revisit the Scripture passage for today's session. This question is designed to help them actively engage the text and then sort out for themselves the connection between what these verses say and the application for how they live their lives as followers of God.

> *Optional follow-up:* As your group closes this study, share one change you plan to make in order to live a life that stands apart from the crowd—a life that is distinct.

LIVE IT OUT

Showing love the way God loves is what makes us truly distinct. Encourage group members to consider the following ways they can stand apart from the rest of the world:

- **Pray.** Commit to pray every day for one person in your life who is difficult to love. Pray that God would bless that person. Notice how your heart softens toward that person.

- **Thank.** Have you ever been difficult to love? Think of someone who loved you during a time when you were hard to love. Make a call and express your thanks for the way his or her love reminded you of the way God loves all the time.

- **Sacrifice.** Jesus loves us sacrificially. What is one practical way you can sacrificially love someone else this week?

Challenge: Jesus is calling us to love in the way He does. That standard of love is unconditional and knows no limits. As you live out this kind of love with others, consider journaling about the impact unconditional love is having on your relationships. You may not recognize the significance until you see the proof on paper.

Pray: As the leader, close this final session of *Distinct* in prayer. Ask the Lord to help each of you love as He loves. Conclude by committing to live lives that stand in sharp contrast to the world. Lives that are distinct.

Note: If you haven't discussed it yet, decide as a group whether or not you plan to continue to meet together and, if so, what Bible study options you would like to pursue. Visit *LifeWay.com/smallgroups* for help, or if you would like more studies like this one, visit *biblestudiesforlife.com/smallgroups.*

My group's prayer requests

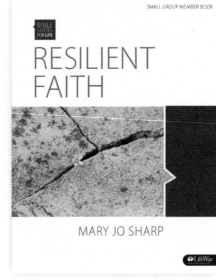
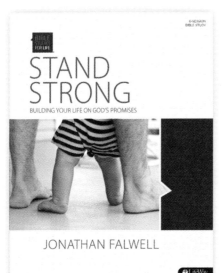
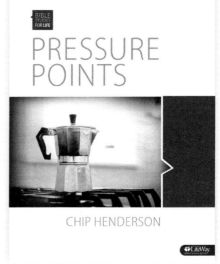